Published by Willow Creek Press, Inc.
P.O. Box 147, Minocqua, Wisconsin 54548

Printed in the United States

DADISMS

WIT, WISDOM & HUMOR

■ WILLOW CREEK PRESS®

"BECAUSE I SAID SO THAT'S WHY!"

-DAD TIP-

Raising kids is part joy and
part guerilla warfare.

-Ed Asner

◆

My daughter's only six months
old and already drawing.
I'd hang it on the fridge but
honestly, it's absolute garbage.

-Ryan Reynolds

◆

I just wake up hoping
I don't screw up today.

-John Krasinski

DID YOU SEE THE DOG'S NEW OUTFIT?

IT WAS QUITE FETCHING!

"FOR PETE'S SAKE!"

"YA KNOW WHEN I WAS A KID..."

A father carries kid pictures
where his money used to be.

-Steve Martin

◆

It doesn't matter who my
father was; it matters who
I remember he was.

-Anne Sexton

◆

Kids are just annoying
short people.

-Hank Azaria

-DAD TIP-

If you're not yelling at your kids, you aren't spending enough time with them.

-Mark Ruffalo

◆

I INVENTED A NEW WORD:

PLAGIARISM!

"WON'T GET VERY FAR WITHOUT THESE!"

(WHEN ALMOST FORGETTING THE CAR KEYS.)

"I'M GOING TO COUNT TO TEN."

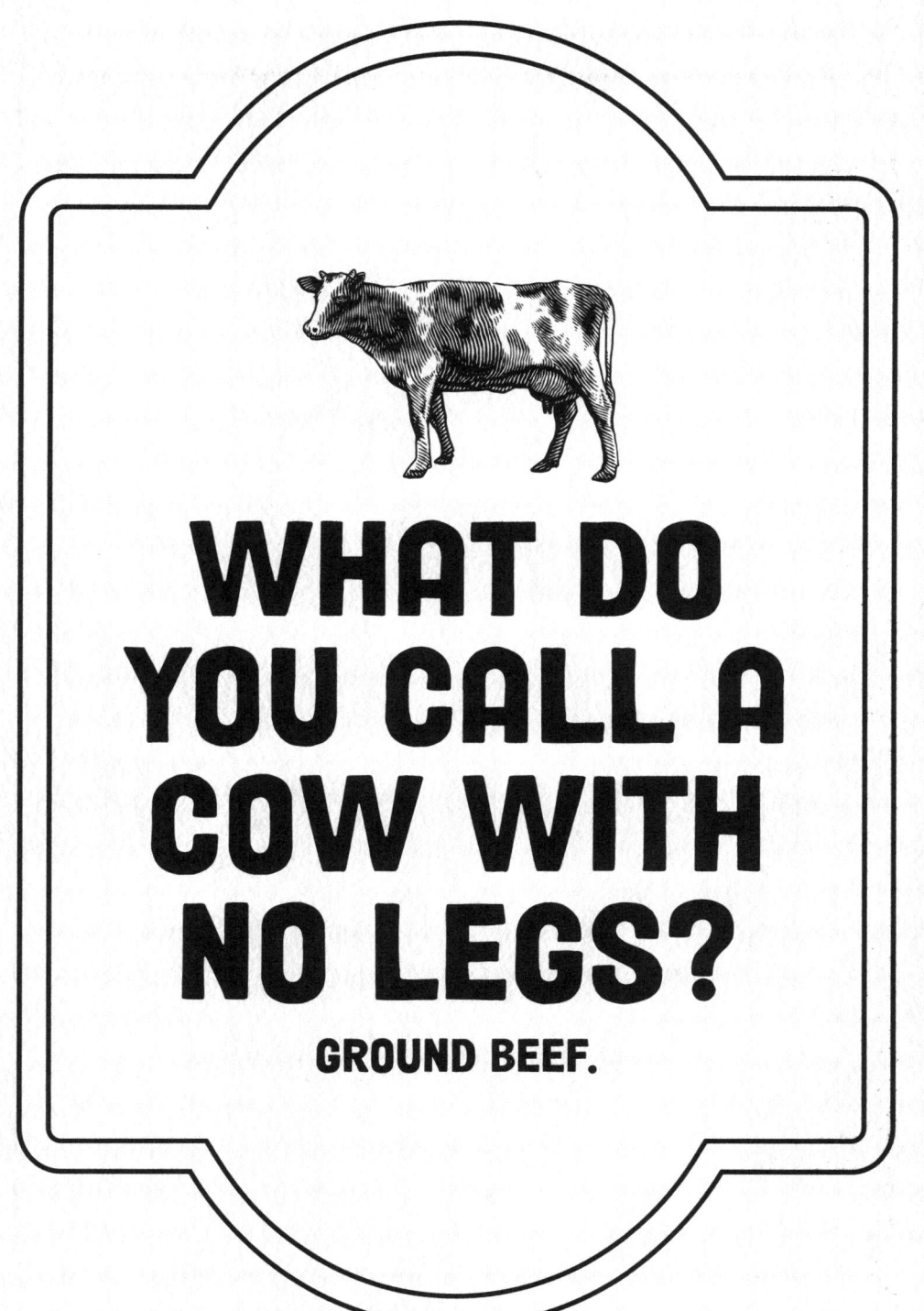

WHAT DO YOU CALL A COW WITH NO LEGS?

GROUND BEEF.

FOUND A SPIDER
IN MY SHOES...
HE LOOKED SILLY. THEY WERE
WAY TOO BIG FOR HIM!

"WHAT'S THE DAMAGE?"

(BEFORE LOOKING AT A BILL.)

"STOP OR I'LL GIVE YOU SOMETHING TO CRY ABOUT."

You can tell what was the best year of your father's life, because they seem to freeze that clothing style and ride it out.

-Jerry Seinfeld

◆

My father had a profound influence on me.
He was a lunatic.

-Spike Milligan

◆

I would rather drink a piping hot bowl of liquid rabies than get on a plane with my two children.

-Ryan Reynolds

HOW DO YOU GET A SQUIRREL TO LIKE YOU?

ACT LIKE YOU'RE NUTS.

"WERE YOU BORN IN A BARN?"

"DID YOU FALL IN?"

(WHEN A KID TAKES TOO LONG IN THE BATHROOM.)

WHAT DO YOU CALL AN ALLIGATOR IN A VEST?

AN INVESTIGATOR.

A two-year-old is like having a blender, but you don't have the top for it.

-Jerry Seinfeld

◆

Booking plane tickets for a family trip is a fun little test to see if I still remember all my kids' birthdays and genders.

-Ken Jennings

◆

-DAD TIP-

Never raise your hand to your kids. It leaves your groin unprotected.

-Red Buttons

"I'M NOT SLEEPING, I'M JUST RESTING MY EYES."

(AFTER FALLING ASLEEP ON THE COUCH.)

"I GUESS THEY LET ANYONE IN HERE."

(WHEN SEEING A FRIEND IN PUBLIC.)

-DAD TIP-

For fatherhood advice, try
to look your child in the eye.
Get to know their name; that
becomes important when
you want something. And
remember to feed them.
That's about all you need.

-Will Ferrell

No one wants to see Dad dance, but he does it anyway.

◆

Nothing is funnier than people without kids telling me how tired they are.

◆

The key to being an awesome dad is aging without maturing.

"MONEY DOESN'T GROW ON TREES."

"WHEN I WAS YOUR AGE..."

HOW WAS ROME SPLIT IN TWO?

WITH A PAIR OF CAESARS.

She got her looks from her father. He's a plastic surgeon.

-Groucho Marx

◆

My mother protected me from the world and my father threatened me with it.

-Quentin Crisp

◆

Fatherhood is all about pretending neckties are the best gifts you ever received.

"IT WAS THE DOG."

(WHEN DAD FARTS.)

"BE CAREFUL WHAT YOU WISH FOR."

I don't have a kid, but I think
I would be a good father.
Especially if my baby
liked to go out drinking.

-Eugene Mirman

———————— ◆ ————————

I asked my old man if I could go
ice-skating on the lake. He told
me, "Wait 'til it gets warmer."

-Rodney Dangerfield

———————— ◆ ————————

-DAD TIP-

Just taught my kids about
taxes by eating 38% of
their ice cream.

-Conan O'Brien

I USED TO HATE FACIAL HAIR.

BUT THEN IT GREW ON ME.

"GLAD WE'RE NOT GOING THAT WAY!"

(WHEN SEEING TRAFFIC ON THE
OTHER SIDE OF THE ROAD.)

"THEY DON'T MAKE 'EM LIKE THEY USED TO."

My dad used to say, "Always fight fire with fire." Which is probably why he got thrown out of the fire brigade.

-Harry Hill

◆

Sometimes I'm amazed that my wife and I created two human beings from scratch yet struggle to assemble the most basic of IKEA cabinets.

-Greg Kinnear

I know when my kids need money because that's when they laugh at my jokes.

◆

Having a conversation while having children is like trying to do your taxes in an inflatable jump house.

◆

My daughter doesn't have any daddy issues, but I can guarantee her boyfriend will.

"IT'S NOT THAT HEAVY. IT'S JUST AWKWARD."

(WHEN LIFTING SOMETHING HEAVY.)

"LET'S ROCK 'N ROLL."

(WHEN IT'S TIME TO LEAVE.)

I WENT ON A ONCE-IN-A-LIFETIME VACATION.

NEVER AGAIN.

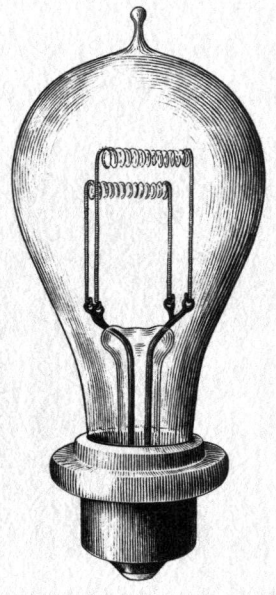

MOST PEOPLE ARE SHOCKED WHEN THEY FIND OUT HOW BAD AN ELECTRICIAN I AM.

"DON'T USE THAT TONE WITH ME."

"I'M NOT JUST TALKING TO HEAR MY OWN VOICE."

For the first two years, being a good dad is mostly about keeping your kid from finding new and creative ways to hurt himself.

◆

Being a dad is when you realize you can actually like people who puke in your car multiple times.

◆

Dad: Spider-killing superhero.

-DAD TIP-

Of course, you'll make a few mistakes. The important thing is that the mistakes you make with your kids are the same ones your parents made with you. At least you know how those turn out.

-Stephen Colbert

"DO YOU THINK I WAS BORN YESTERDAY?"

"GO ASK YOUR MOTHER."

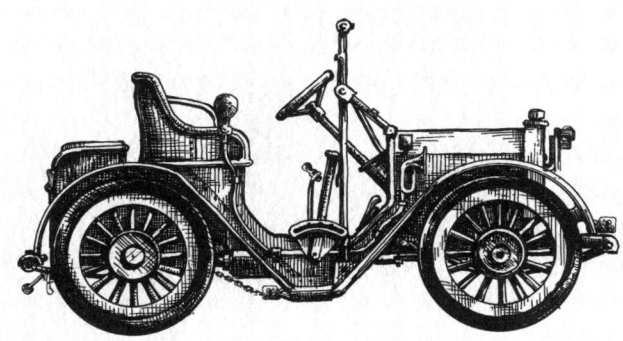

MY CAR ONLY WORKS EVERY OTHER DAY.

I THINK IT MIGHT BE THE ALTERNATOR.

A man's children and his garden
both reflect the amount of
weeding done during the
growing season.

———————◆———————

One night a father overheard
his son pray: Dear God, make
me the kind of man my Daddy
is. Later that night, the father
prayed, Dear God, make me
the kind of man my son
wants me to be.

"FOUND IT!"

(WHILE POINTING A STUD FINDER AT HIS CHEST.)

"YOU DON'T KNOW WHAT HARD WORK IS."

If you have never been hated by your child, you have never been a parent.

-Bette Davis

◆

Hallelujah! Where's the Tylenol?

-Clark Griswold

◆

-DAD TIP-

A child, like your stomach, doesn't need all you can afford to give it.

-Frank A. Clark

TODAY I GAVE MY DEAD BATTERIES AWAY.

THEY WERE FREE OF CHARGE.

"I'LL TURN THIS CAR AROUND!"

"WELL, THE LAWN ISN'T GOING TO MOW ITSELF."

Before I got married I had six
theories about raising children;
now I have six children
and no theories.

-John Wilmot

A father is a banker
provided by nature.

-French proverb

I cannot think of any need in
children as strong as the need
for a father's protection.

-Sigmund Freud

SCIENTISTS HAVE JUST COMPLETED A STUDY INTO THE EFFECTS OF ALCOHOL ON WALKING.

THE RESULT WAS STAGGERING.

"WE NEEDED THIS RAIN."

(EVERY TIME IT RAINS.)

"GUESS IT'S FREE THEN."

(WHEN A CASHIER HAS TROUBLE SCANNING AN ITEM.)

MY UNCLE WAS CRUSHED BY A PIANO....

HIS FUNERAL WAS VERY LOW KEY.

They vomit a lot. For a second
I thought I need to rename my
first Linda Blair and hire a
priest because she was
spitting up so much.

-Jimmy Fallon

◆

Fatherhood is great
because you can ruin
someone from scratch.

-Jon Stewart

◆

Parenting is like a cult. And as a
cult member, you try to explain
it to other people, but we just
appear like lunatics.

-Jim Gaffigan

"YOU'RE GROUNDED 'TIL YOU'RE THIRTY."

"HOW MANY TIMES DO I HAVE TO SAY IT?"

-DAD TIP-

Buying your kid a goldfish
is a great way to teach
them responsibility for
24 to 36 hours.

-Conan O'Brien

◆

There should be a children's
song, "if you're happy and
you know it keep it to
yourself and let dad sleep."

-Jim Gaffigan

HOW MANY TICKLES DOES IT TAKE TO MAKE AN OCTOPUS LAUGH?

10–TICKLES.

"IF SOMEONE TOLD YOU TO JUMP OFF A CLIFF, WOULD YOU DO IT?"

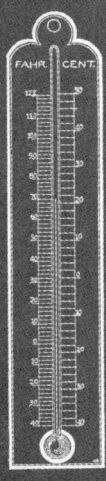

"I'M NOT PAYING TO HEAT THE WHOLE NEIGHBORHOOD."
(WHEN THE DOOR IS LEFT OPEN.)

WHAT DID THE BUFFALO SAY TO HER CHILD AS HE LEFT FOR SCHOOL?

BISON.

Dad taught me everything
I know. Unfortunately,
he didn't teach me
everything he knows.

-Al Unser, Sr.

◆

There are three stages of a
man's life: he believes in Santa
Claus, he doesn't believe in
Santa Claus, he is Santa Claus.

◆

He didn't tell me how to live;
he lived, and let me watch
him do it.

-Clarence Budington Kelland

"PEOPLE DON'T KNOW HOW TO DRIVE IN THIS TOWN."

(IN EVERY TOWN YOU'RE IN.)

"I GUESS WE'LL HAVE TO AMPUTATE."

(TO A KID WITH A MINOR CUT.)

If you must hold yourself up to your children as an object lesson, hold yourself up as a warning and not as an example.

-George Bernard Shaw

◆

The joys of parents are secret, and so are their griefs and fears.

-Francis Bacon, Sr.

◆

If I chance to talk a little wild, forgive me; I had it from my father.

-William Shakespeare

WHAT DO YOU GET WHEN THE QUEEN OF ENGLAND FARTS?

A NOBLE GAS.

"WHEN YOU PAY THE RENT, YOU CAN MAKE THE RULES."

"AND THAT'S HOW THEY GET YOU."

(AFTER DECLINING ADDITIONAL WARRANTY PROTECTION.)

Don't worry that children
never listen to you; worry
that they are always
watching you.

-Robert Fulghum

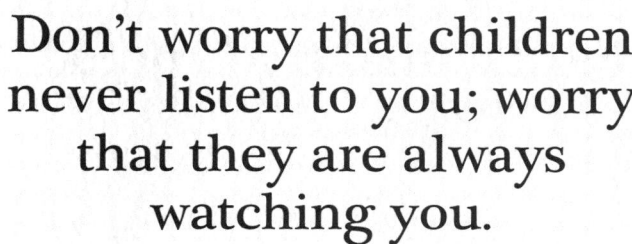

-DAD TIP-

If your child is crying, hold
it and whisper: "You don't
have a clue what horrors
this world holds."

-Rob Delaney

Likely as not, the child you can do the least with will do the most to make you proud.

-Mignon McLaughlin

♦

His heritage to his children wasn't words or possessions, but an unspoken treasure— the treasure of his example as a man and a father.

-Will Rodgers

♦

The most important thing a father can do for his children is to love their mother.

"DON'T MAKE THAT FACE, IT'LL GET STUCK LIKE THAT."

"NO, YOUR OTHER RIGHT."

(WHEN SOMEONE MISTAKES LEFT FOR RIGHT.)

WHAT KIND OF SHOES DOES A FROG WEAR?

OPEN TOAD.

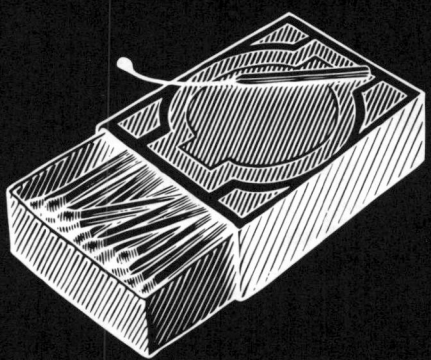

I JOINED
A DATING
SITE FOR
ARSONISTS.
I'VE BEEN GETTING
A LOT OF MATCHES.

"NO, I GOT ALL OF 'EM CUT."

(WHEN ASKED IF HE GOT A HAIRCUT.)

"JEEZ LOUISE!"

Put the baby in her crib tonight.
She scrunched her nose, giggled,
and turned into a thousand bats.

-Ryan Reynolds

◆

Now that I'm a parent, I
understand why my father
was in a bad mood a lot.

-Adam Sandler

◆

My father would take me to
the playground and put
me on mood swings.

-Jay London

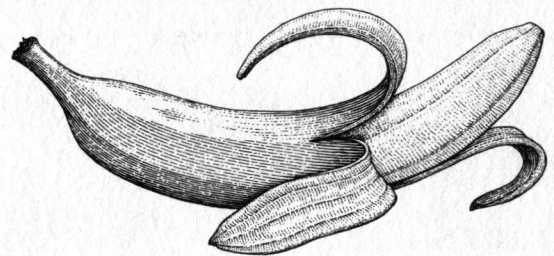

WHY DID THE BANANA GO TO THE DOCTOR?

BECAUSE IT WASN'T PEELING WELL.

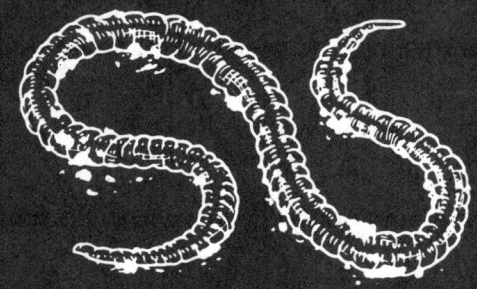

"THE EARLY BIRD GETS THE WORM."

"THAT'S NOT GOING ANYWHERE."

(AFTER TYING SOMETHING DOWN.)

I rescind my early statement that I could never fall in love with a girl who regularly poops her pants. I hadn't met my daughter yet.

-Dax Shepard

◆

How come my three-year-old son can remember every species and genus of dinosaur and I can't even remember my own phone number?

-Taye Diggs

When you have brought up kids, there are memories you store directly in your tear ducts.

-Robert Brault

◆

A man never stands as tall as when he kneels to help a child.

-Knights of Pythagoras

◆

"I have found the best way to give advice to your children is to find out what they want and then advise them to do it."

-Harry Truman

"DON'T MAKE ME COME UP THERE!"

"I'M NOT YOUR CHAUFFEUR."

I remember the time I was kidnapped and they sent a piece of my finger to my father. He said he wanted more proof.

-Rodney Dangerfield

———◆———

Hey, hey, kids. Everybody in the car. Boat leaves in two minutes. Or perhaps you don't want to see the second largest ball of twine on the face of the earth, which is only four short hours away?

-Clark Griswold

WHERE DO YOU LEARN TO MAKE ICE CREAM?

SUNDAE SCHOOL.

"YOU MAKE A BETTER DOOR THAN A WINDOW!"

"YOU CALL THAT RACKET MUSIC?"

If the only objective of parenting was to raise really loud kids, I'd be killing it.

-Jim Gaffigan

———— ◆ ————

The trouble with having a stubbornness contest with your kids is that they have your stubbornness gene.

-Robert Brault

———— ◆ ————

My kids always ask me which one of them is my favorite. I don't tell them I don't actually like any of them.

A good father is one of the
most unsung, unpraised,
unnoticed, and yet one
of the most valuable
assets in our society.

-Billy Graham

——————◆——————

If the past cannot teach the
present and the father cannot
teach the son, then history need
not have bothered to go on,
and the world wasted a
great deal of time.

-Russell Hoban

"PULL MY FINGER."

"WHY PAY MONEY FOR JEANS THAT ALREADY HAVE HOLES?"

I JUST WATCHED A PROGRAM ABOUT BEAVERS.

IT WAS THE BEST DAM PROGRAM I'VE EVER SEEN!

Sometimes the poorest man
leaves his children the
richest inheritance.

-Ruth E. Renkel

◆

"Having children is like living
in a frat house. Nobody sleeps,
everything's broken and
there's a lot of throwing up."

-Ray Romano

◆

"You know what it's like
having a fourth kid? Imagine
you're drowning, then
someone hands you a baby."

-Jim Gaffigan

"I'M NOT GOING TO TELL YOU AGAIN!"

"WORKING HARD OR HARDLY WORKING?"

DID YOU HEAR ABOUT THE SENSITIVE BURGLAR?

HE TAKES THINGS PERSONALLY.

WHY DID THE LION EAT THE TIGHTROPE WALKER?

HE WANTED A WELL–BALANCED MEAL.

"ACT YOUR AGE AND NOT YOUR SHOE SIZE."

"YOU'RE GOING OUT IN THAT?"

(WHEN HIS DAUGHTER IS WEARING REVEALING CLOTHING.)

Raising kids may be a thankless job with ridiculous hours, but at least the pay sucks.

-Jim Gaffigan

◆

Children are a great comfort in your old age—and they help you reach it faster, too.

-Lionel Kauffman

◆

Went to Disneyland because my daughter's obsessed with Mickey Mouse. She was so excited when I got home and told her.

-Ryan Reynolds

No matter which kids' book I read to my screaming baby on an airplane, the moral of the story is always something about a vasectomy.

-Ryan Reynolds

◆

A father is a man who expects his son to be as good a man as he meant to be.

-Frank A. Clark

◆

My four-year-old son gave me a handmade card for Father's Day. Maybe for Christmas I'll draw him a picture of some toys.

-Jim Gaffigan

"DON'T SPEND IT ALL IN ONE PLACE."